50 fixes FOR BROWNIE MIXES

50 fixes FOR BROWNIE MIXES

AIMEE BERRETT

FRONT TABLE BOOKS | AN IMPRINT OF CEDAR FORT, INC.
SPRINGVILLE, UTAH

ISBN 13: 978-1-4621-1742-0

Published by Front Table Books, an imprint of Cedar Fort, Inc.
2373 W. 700 S., Springville, UT 84663
Distributed by Cedar Fort, Inc., www.cedarfort.com

LIBRARY OF CONGRESS CATALOGING-IN-PUBLICATION

Berrett, Aimee, 1988- author.
50 fixes for brownie mixes / Aimee Berrett.
    pages cm
Includes index.
ISBN 978-1-4621-1742-0 (layflat binding : alk. paper)
1. Brownies (Cooking) I. Title. II. Title: Fifty fixes for brownie mixes.
TX771.B473 2016
641.86'53--dc23
                    2015028092

Cover design by Sarah K. Crane
Interior design by M. Shaun McMurdie and Rebecca J. Greenwood
Cover design © 2016 by Cedar Fort, Inc.
Edited by Jessica Romrell

Printed in the United States of America

10 9 8 7 6 5 4 3 2 1

Printed on acid-free paper

To my husband and my mom, who have been my biggest cheerleaders along the way. And to all the fans of *Like Mother, Like Daughter*, I couldn't have done it without you.

Contents

Decadent BROWNIES

BROWNIE *Batter Desserts*

BROWNIE *Mix-Ins*

Other BROWNIE *Delights*

Acknowledgments

I could not have written this book alone. A huge thanks to our blog readers and fans. I wouldn't have a blog or a cookbook without you and I thank you from my whole heart.

Thank you to my mom for joining me in the blogging journey, and to my dad for always teaching me to be a hard worker. Thank you to my other family members and friends for always loving, supporting, and encouraging me.

Thank you to countless neighbors, friends, and coworkers for being the best taste testers.

And the biggest thank you to my wonderful husband for supporting me along the way, joining me in gaining some extra pounds each as we taste-tested recipe after recipe, making last-minute trips to the store for me when I needed more ingredients, and most of all, just being there for me and being my biggest fan the whole way through.

Introduction

Hi! I am **Aimee Berrett**, the co-founder and co-blogger of the site *Like Mother, Like Daughter*. I thought of the idea for this cookbook based on a post on my blog for 15 ways to jazz up boxed brownies. The post has been the most popular post on my blog since I wrote it over 4 years ago and helped me to know that I'm not the only one obsessed with boxed brownies.

This cookbook contains 50 amazing, tried-and-true, tested and retested recipes. I have always loved boxed mix brownies, and every one of these recipes starts with your favorite brownie box mix. Boxed brownies have always been one of my favorite desserts, especially when I am in a time crunch, and this cookbook helps to take those delicious treats to the next level.

In this book you will find everything from the traditional bar brownies topped with things like strawberry buttercream and chocolate, or swirled with a cheesecake filling, to brownie batter desserts, like ice cream and fudge, to desserts where your favorite brownie is rolled into little balls and baked in a cookie. I hope you love all of these recipes as much as I do, and I hope you have as much fun baking and eating them as I did.

I hope that with these recipes you will be able to make an amazing dessert that your whole family will love, that you can share with friends or coworkers, or even take to a school bake sale (no one will know that you made it from a mix!). These recipes are all not only delicious, but quick and easy so you will not be spending hours slaving in the kitchen, but instead enjoying time with your family, reading a book, or cooking other delicious recipes. I hope this book will become one of your go-to sources for a quick and easy dessert that you and friends and family will all love!

I am so grateful for all the supportive people in my life and wouldn't be here with a cookbook if it weren't for all of you. I hope you enjoy it as much as I enjoyed writing it!

If you are joining me in this cooking and baking journey for the first time I hope you will come visit me at our blog, *Like Mother, Like Daughter* (www.lmld.org), soon for more easy and delicious recipes!

Decadent
BROWNIES

ALMOND JOY *Brownies*

These brownies have the same great taste of Almond Joy candy bars—but in delicious brownie form. With a creamy sweet coconut layer, almonds, and a chocolate ganache, this is a brownie that coconut lovers will go crazy for!

Serves · 15–18

1 (18-oz.) box brownie mix
additional ingredients as listed on back of brownie mix (eggs, oil, water)

FOR THE COCONUT LAYER:

3 cups shredded sweetened coconut

¾ cup sweetened condensed milk

1½ cups powdered sugar

¼ cup almonds

FOR THE CHOCOLATE GANACHE:

1 cup chocolate chips

5 Tbsp. butter

PREHEAT OVEN, PREPARE BROWNIE BATTER, and bake brownies in a greased 9 × 13 pan according to package directions. Remove from oven and allow brownies to cool completely.

In a medium-sized bowl, stir together coconut, sweetened condensed milk, and powdered sugar. Use a wet spatula or wet fingers to spread coconut mixture over brownie top. Place almonds evenly over coconut mixture.

Melt chocolate chips and butter in a small bowl in microwave in 20-second increments, stirring after each increment until smooth. It should take 40–60 seconds total. Pour chocolate ganache over coconut layer and spread evenly. Allow chocolate to set before slicing, or place brownies in fridge to chill quicker before slicing.

BETTER THAN ANYTHING
Brownies

Instead of the usual cake form, try these Better than Anything Brownies. The same great flavors in a new style: a moist caramel brownie topped with whipped cream and crunchy toffee pieces.

Serves · 15–18

1 (18-oz.) box brownie mix
additional ingredients as listed on back of brownie mix (eggs, oil, water)

1 extra egg (for cake-like brownies)

FOR THE TOPPING:

½ cup sweetened condensed milk

½ cup caramel ice cream topping

1 (8-oz.) container Cool Whip, or 2 cups whipped cream

½ cup Heath chocolate toffee baking bits

PREHEAT OVEN AND PREPARE BROWNIE BATTER ACCORDING TO PACKAGE DIRECTIONS for cake-like brownies. Bake in a greased 9 × 13 pan according to package directions. Remove brownies from oven and allow to cool for 5 minutes.

In a medium-sized bowl, combine sweetened condensed milk and caramel topping. Poke all over brownie top with a fork, knife, or toothpick. Pour caramel mixture over brownies. Tilt pan slightly as needed to get caramel mixture to cover entire brownie top. Put brownies in fridge for 1 hour.

Spread Cool Whip evenly over brownie top. Sprinkle with toffee bits evenly over Cool Whip. Place back in fridge and allow to chill for another hour (or up to overnight) before serving.

BUCKEYE *Brownies*

These rich brownies are topped with a creamy homemade peanut butter buttercream frosting and chocolate ganache. Be sure to eat these delectable treats with a big glass of milk!

Serves · 15–18

1 (18-oz.) box brownie mix
additional ingredients as listed on back of brownie mix (eggs, oil, water)

FOR THE PEANUT BUTTER LAYER:

½ cup butter, softened

1 cup creamy peanut butter

¼ tsp. salt

3 cups powdered sugar

1 tsp. vanilla extract

3 Tbsp. milk

FOR THE CHOCOLATE PEANUT BUTTER GANACHE:

1 cup chocolate chips

¼ cup creamy peanut butter

PREHEAT OVEN, PREPARE BROWNIE BATTER, and bake brownies in a greased 9 × 13 pan according to package directions. Remove from oven and allow brownies to cool completely.

In a medium-sized bowl, cream together butter, peanut butter, and salt for a couple of minutes until light and creamy. Add in powdered sugar, vanilla, and milk. Mix until smooth. Add in a little more powdered sugar or a little more milk if needed to get a spreadable consistency for frosting. Spread peanut butter frosting over cooled brownies.

Melt chocolate chips and peanut butter in a small bowl in microwave in 30-second increments, stirring after each increment until smooth. It should take about 1 minute to be smooth. Pour chocolate peanut butter ganache over peanut butter layer and spread evenly. Allow ganache to set before slicing, or place brownies in fridge to chill quicker before slicing.

Candy Bar BROWNIES

Personalize these candy bar brownies by using pieces of your favorite candy bars!

Serves · 15–18

1 (18-oz.) box brownie mix

additional ingredients as listed on back of brownie mix (eggs, oil, water)

1 cup chopped candy bar pieces (about 8 fun size bars), divided

PREHEAT OVEN AND PREPARE BROWNIE MIX according to package directions.

Pour half of brownie batter into a greased 9 × 13 baking pan. Sprinkle half of candy bar pieces over batter. Pour remaining brownie batter over the top (it might not cover candy bar pieces completely). Sprinkle remaining candy bar pieces over the top, spreading them evenly.

Bake for 30–35 minutes, until an inserted toothpick comes out mostly clean.

Remove from oven. Allow to cool and then slice and serve.

Cheesecake Swirl
BROWNIES

These rich and decadent brownies have a delicious and creamy cheesecake swirl throughout, making an indulgent and irresistible treat.

Serves · 15–18

1 (18-oz.) box brownie mix
additional ingredients as listed on back of brownie mix (eggs, oil, water)

FOR THE CHEESECAKE SWIRL:

1½ (8-oz.) pkgs. (or 12-oz.) softened cream cheese, or Neufchatel cream cheese

1 large egg

1 Tbsp. flour

½ cup sugar

½ tsp. vanilla extract

PREHEAT OVEN AND PREPARE BROWNIE MIX ACCORDING TO PACKAGE DIRECTIONS. Set aside.

In a medium-sized bowl, beat cream cheese for 1–2 minutes until smooth and creamy. Add in egg, flour, sugar, and vanilla. Stir mixture until combined.

Pour and spread all but about 1/2 cup of brownie batter into a greased 9 × 13 pan. Spoon cream cheese mixture on top of brownie batter. Spoon remaining brownie batter on top of cream cheese mixture. Using a knife, swirl cream cheese and brownie batter together, creating a marbled effect.

Place in preheated oven and bake for 35–40 minutes, or until a toothpick inserted near the middle comes out mostly clean. Remove from oven and allow to cool completely before cutting into pieces.

PEPPERMINT BARK
Brownies

These brownies taste just like peppermint bark. They are topped with rich layers of chocolate and white chocolate infused with peppermint extract for a minty treat!

Serves • 15–18

1 (18-oz.) box brownie mix

additional ingredients as listed on back of brownie mix (eggs, oil, water)

FOR THE TOPPING:

1 cup semisweet chocolate chips

½ tsp. peppermint extract, divided

1 cup white chocolate chips

¼ cup crushed peppermint candy canes

PREHEAT OVEN, PREPARE BROWNIE BATTER, AND BAKE BROWNIES in a greased 9 x 13 pan according to package directions. Remove from oven and allow brownies to cool completely.

Melt semisweet chocolate chips in a small bowl in microwave in 20-second increments until smooth, about 1 minute total. Stir in ¼ teaspoon peppermint extract. Pour melted chocolate chips over brownies and spread evenly. Repeat with white chocolate. Sprinkle crushed candy cane pieces over the top. Allow to cool completely before slicing and serving.

CHOCOLATE-COVERED STRAWBERRY *Brownies*

These brownies have the great taste of chocolate-covered strawberries with a layer of brownies, topped with a strawberry buttercream and chocolate ganache, and covered with homemade chocolate-covered strawberries for a decadent and delicious dessert.

Serves · 15–18

1 (18-oz.) box brownie mix
additional ingredients as listed
on back of brownie mix (eggs, oil,
water)

FOR THE STRAWBERRY
BUTTERCREAM FROSTING:

1 cup chopped strawberries

½ cup butter (1 stick),
softened

3 cups powdered sugar

1 tsp. vanilla extract

FOR THE CHOCOLATE GANACHE:

1 cup chocolate chips

5 Tbsp. butter

FOR THE CHOCOLATE-COVERED
STRAWBERRIES (OPTIONAL):

1 cup chocolate chips

½ Tbsp. coconut oil

15–20 strawberries

PREHEAT OVEN, PREPARE BROWNIE BATTER,
AND BAKE BROWNIES in a greased 9 × 13 pan
according to package directions. Remove from
oven and allow brownies to cool completely.

FOR STRAWBERRY BUTTERCREAM FROSTING:
Puree strawberries in a blender or food
processor. Strain strawberry juice through a
fine mesh strainer to remove most seeds. Cook
in a small pot over medium heat until juice has
been reduced by about half. (This will make the
strawberry flavor stronger.) This takes about
5 minutes and yields about 2 tablespoons juice.
In a large bowl, beat butter until creamy. Add in
powdered sugar, strawberry juice, and vanilla.
Beat until light and fluffy. Spread mixture evenly
over cooled brownies.

FOR GANACHE: Melt chocolate chips and butter
in a small bowl in microwave in 20-second
increments, stirring after each increment until
smooth, about 1 minute total. Pour chocolate
ganache over strawberry buttercream frosting,
spreading to cover evenly.

FOR CHOCOLATE-COVERED STRAWBERRIES:
Melt chocolate chips and coconut oil in a small
microwavable bowl in 20-second increments,
stirring after each increment until smooth,
about 1 minute total. Dip each strawberry into
chocolate and place on a cookie sheet lined with
waxed paper. Place in fridge for a few minutes
until chocolate is hard.

Top ganache with chocolate-covered strawberries.
Arrange so that there will be 1 strawberry per
brownie piece when sliced, and place brownies
in fridge to chill for 1 hour. (Or add chocolate-
covered strawberries after ganache is hardened
when serving). Slice into pieces and serve.

COOKIES AND CREAM
Brownies

Both the brownies and the buttercream frosting of this dessert are made with chocolate crème-filled cookies for the perfect cookies and cream taste. Be sure to serve them with milk!

Serves · 12–16

1 (18-oz.) box brownie mix

additional ingredients as listed on back of brownie mix (eggs, oil, water)

12–16 chocolate crème-filled cookies

FOR THE FROSTING:

½ cup butter, softened

3 cups powdered sugar

1 tsp. vanilla extract

2–3 Tbsp. milk

20 chocolate crème filled cookies

PREHEAT OVEN AND PREPARE BROWNIE MIX according to package directions. Pour half of batter into a greased 9 × 9 or 11 × 7 pan. Place chocolate crème-filled cookies on top of batter. Pour remaining batter carefully over cookies. Bake brownies according to package directions, or until a toothpick comes out mostly clean. Remove from oven and allow brownies to cool completely.

In a medium-sized bowl, cream together butter and powdered sugar. Add in vanilla and milk and then stir until a soft frosting is formed. Roughly chop and crush chocolate cookies and fold them into frosting. Spread frosting over brownies. Slice into pieces and serve.

Cosmic BROWNIES

These rich brownies are dense and chocolatey, topped with a rich chocolate ganache and rainbow chip crunch sprinkles! They'll be perfect for children and adults alike!

Serves · 15–18

1 (18-oz.) box brownie mix

eggs and water as listed on back of brownie mix

butter (instead of the oil called for on the box, use the same amount of butter)

1 Tbsp. cornstarch

FOR THE GANACHE:

1 cup semisweet chocolate chips

½ cup milk chocolate chips

½ cup heavy cream

2 Tbsp. rainbow chip crunch sprinkles *

PREHEAT OVEN ACCORDING TO DIRECTIONS on the back of the brownie mix. Mix together brownie mix, eggs, water, butter, and cornstarch. Pour batter into a greased 9 × 13 pan and bake according to package directions, until a toothpick comes out mostly clean. Remove from oven and allow brownies to cool for 5 minutes.

In a medium-sized bowl, combine semisweet chocolate chips, milk chocolate chips and heavy cream. Microwave in 30-second increments, stirring after each until ganache is smooth, about 1 minute total. Pour ganache over brownie top and spread evenly. Sprinkle rainbow chips over ganache. Allow ganache to cool completely before slicing and serving, or place brownies in fridge to chill quicker before slicing

* Rainbow chip crunch sprinkles can be ordered online, or found at most craft stores. Or you can use mini M&M's or chocolate-covered sunflower seeds instead.

Cookie Dough BROWNIES

A rich layer of cookie dough on top of brownies and topped with a buttery chocolate ganache.

Serves · 15–18

1 (18-oz.) box brownie mix
additional ingredients as listed on back of brownie mix (eggs, oil, water)

FOR THE COOKIE DOUGH:

1½ sticks butter (¾ cup), melted

¾ cup brown sugar

½ cup sugar

1 tsp. vanilla extract

2 Tbsp. milk

1½ cups flour

½ tsp. salt

1 cup mini chocolate chips

FOR THE CHOCOLATE GANACHE:

1 cup chocolate chips

4 Tbsp. butter

PREHEAT OVEN, PREPARE BROWNIE BATTER, AND BAKE BROWNIES in a greased 9 × 13 pan according to package directions. Remove from oven and allow brownies to cool completely.

FOR THE COOKIE DOUGH: In a medium-sized bowl, beat melted butter and sugars for about 2 minutes until light and creamy. Add in vanilla extract and milk. Stir in. Add in flour and salt. Mix until combined. Fold in chocolate chips. Carefully using your hands, spread cookie dough over cooled brownies.

FOR GANACHE: Melt chocolate chips and butter in a small bowl in microwave in 30-second increments, stirring after each increment until smooth, for about 1 minute total. Pour chocolate ganache over cookie dough and spread evenly. Place brownies in fridge to chill for 1 hour before slicing and serving.

GERMAN CHOCOLATE
Brownies

These brownies are topped with a homemade coconut pecan frosting and drizzled with chocolate for a delicious and rich taste.

Serves · 15–18

1 (18-oz.) box brownie mix
additional ingredients as listed on back of brownie mix (eggs, oil, water)

1 extra egg (for cake-like brownies)

FOR THE COCONUT PECAN FROSTING:

3 egg yolks

1¼ tsp. vanilla extract

1 cup + 2 Tbsp. evaporated milk

1 cup + 2 Tbsp. sugar

½ cup butter (1 stick)

1½ cups shredded sweetened coconut (shredded coconut—not flakes)

1 cup chopped pecans

FOR THE CHOCOLATE DRIZZLE:

½ cup chocolate chips

PREHEAT OVEN, PREPARE BROWNIE BATTER, and bake brownies in a greased 9 x 13 pan according to package directions for cake-like brownies. Remove from oven and allow brownies to cool completely.

FOR COCONUT PECAN FROSTING: In a medium-sized saucepan, beat together egg yolks, vanilla, and evaporated milk until well blended. Add sugar and butter, and then heat on medium-high heat for about 15 minutes until thickened and golden brown. Stir constantly for the last 10 minutes once mixture is boiling. After mixture is a thick golden brown, mix in the coconut flakes and pecans. Remove from stove top. Allow frosting to cool for about 5 minutes before pouring on top of brownies and spreading evenly. Allow to cool completely.

FOR CHOCOLATE DRIZZLE : Melt chocolate chips in a small bowl in microwave in 30-second increments, stirring after each increment until smooth, about 1 minute total. Put melted chocolate into a small ziplock bag. Clip the corner of the ziplock bag and drizzle chocolate over brownie top. Let chocolate harden and then slice up and serve.

23

MEXICAN *Brownies*

These brownies have a delightful spicy kick with the addition of cayenne pepper and cinnamon. A delicious whipped cream topping cools the flavor down to perfection.

Serves · 15–18

1 (18-oz.) box brownie mix
additional ingredients as listed
on back of brownie mix (eggs, oil,
water)

1 tsp. cinnamon

¼ tsp. cayenne pepper

FOR THE WHIPPED CREAM

2 cups heavy cream

2 Tbsp. sugar

½ tsp. cinnamon

PREHEAT OVEN ACCORDING TO DIRECTIONS on brownie mix. Mix together brownie mix, eggs oil, water, cinnamon, and cayenne pepper. Pour batter into a greased 9 × 13 pan and bake according to package directions. Remove from oven and allow brownies to cool completely.

When you're ready to serve, add heavy cream and sugar to a medium-sized bowl and whisk quickly until stiff peaks form. Spread whipped cream over brownie top. Sprinkle with cinnamon. Slice and serve.

S'MORES *Brownies*

Get the same great taste of s'mores in these brownies. They have a graham cracker crust and are topped with marshmallows to give them those great flavors!

Serves · 15–18

1 (18-oz.) box brownie mix

additional ingredients as listed on back of brownie mix (eggs, oil, water)

6–8 full graham crackers, divided

2½ cups mini marshmallows

¼ cup chocolate chips

PREHEAT OVEN AND PREPARE BROWNIE BATTER according to package directions. Line a greased 9 x 13 pan with graham crackers. If needed, break crackers into pieces to cover entire pan. Pour brownie batter on top of graham crackers. Bake according to package directions.

Sprinkle mini marshmallows and chocolate chips on top of brownies. Break up 1 graham cracker into small pieces and sprinkle it over marshmallows and chocolate chips.

Put brownies back in oven and change heat to broil. Bake for an additional 1–2 minutes, watching brownies closely to prevent burning. Remove from oven when marshmallows are golden.

Allow brownies to cool before slicing.

Mint BROWNIES

Top your brownies with a refreshing mint frosting and chocolate ganache for a delicious mint chocolate treat!

Serves • 15–18

1 (18-oz.) box brownie mix

additional ingredients as listed on back of brownie mix (eggs, oil, water)

FOR THE MINT FROSTING:

½ cup butter (1 stick), softened

2½ cups powdered sugar

2 Tbsp. milk

1 tsp. peppermint extract

3 drops green food coloring

FOR THE CHOCOLATE GANACHE:

1 cup chocolate chips

5 Tbsp. butter

PREHEAT OVEN, PREPARE BROWNIE BATTER, AND BAKE BROWNIES in a greased 9 × 13 pan according to package directions. Remove from oven and allow brownies to cool completely.

FOR MINT FROSTING: In a medium-sized bowl, beat softened butter until smooth, light, and creamy, about 2 minutes. Add in powdered sugar, milk, peppermint extract, and food coloring. Beat on high for 1–2 minutes. Spread frosting over brownie top evenly.

FOR CHOCOLATE GANACHE: Melt chocolate chips and butter in a small bowl in microwave in 20-second increments, stirring after each increment until smooth, about 1 minute total. Pour chocolate ganache over mint layer, spreading to cover evenly.

Place brownies in fridge to chill for 1 hour. Slice and serve.

MICROWAVE MUG
Brownies

When that chocolate craving strikes, this microwave mug brownie is the perfect solution! It only takes 2 minutes to make the perfect chocolatey treat. Top with ice cream or whipped cream to make it even more decadent.

Serves · 1

½ cup brownie mix (not prepared)

3 Tbsp. water

1 Tbsp. mini chocolate chips (optional)

OPTIONAL TOPPINGS:

vanilla ice cream

whipped cream

MIX TOGETHER BROWNIE MIX AND WATER IN A MUG that is approximately 8 oz. (anywhere from 6–10 oz. is okay). Stir in chocolate chips if desired.

Microwave for about 90 seconds until brownie looks cooked. Microwave in additional 15-second increments if needed. Allow to set for 30 seconds.

Top with ice cream or whipped cream and enjoy.

RASPBERRY NUTELLA
Brownies

These brownies are swirled with raspberry preserves and Nutella for rich chocolate and berry flavor.

Serves · 18

1 (18-oz.) box brownie mix

additional ingredients as listed on back of brownie mix (eggs, oil, water)

²/₃ cup fresh raspberries

3 Tbsp. sugar

6 Tbsp. Nutella

PREHEAT OVEN, PREPARE BROWNIE BATTER, and place in a greased 9 × 13 pan according to package directions. Do not bake yet.

In a large bowl, smash raspberries until all big chunks are gone and a puree texture is reached. Mix in sugar.

Microwave Nutella for 20 seconds until it's extra creamy.

Spoon raspberry mixture and Nutella, separately, by tablespoonfuls on top of the brownie batter. Alternate with each to have them spaced evenly. Swirl gently with a knife to create a marbled effect.

Place in oven and bake for 30–35 minutes, until a toothpick inserted comes out mostly clean. Allow to cool completely before cutting and serving.

PUMPKIN *Brownies*

These brownies are only 3 ingredients for a chocolate pumpkin dessert perfect for fall, or anytime of the year.

Serves · 15–18

1 (18-oz.) box brownie mix

1 (14-oz.) can pumpkin puree

1 tsp. pumpkin spice

PREHEAT THE OVEN TO 350 DEGREES. In a medium-sized bowl, mix the brownie mix, pumpkin puree, and pumpkin spice. Pour the brownie batter into a greased 9 × 13 pan. Bake brownies for about 35 minutes, until an inserted toothpick comes out clean.

Allow brownies to cool completely. Sprinkle top with powdered sugar if desired. Slice and serve.

Red Velvet BROWNIES

These rich red velvet brownies are topped with a smooth cream cheese frosting. They're delicious and the red color makes them perfect for Valentine's Day, Christmas, or any day of the year.

Serves · 15–18

1 (18-oz.) box brownie mix

Eggs and oil as listed
on back of brownie mix

Milk (instead of water called for
on the box, use the same amount
of milk)

1 tsp. vinegar

1 Tbsp. red food coloring

FOR THE CREAM CHEESE FROSTING:

1 (8-oz.) pkg. softened cream
cheese

½ cup butter (1 stick),
room temperature

1½ cups powdered sugar

1 tsp. vanilla extract

PREHEAT OVEN AND MIX TOGETHER BROWNIE MIX, eggs, oil, milk, vinegar, and food coloring. Pour batter into a greased 9 × 13 pan and bake according to package directions. Remove from oven and allow brownies to cool completely.

Put cream cheese in a large mixing bowl and whisk until smooth. Add in butter, 2 tablespoons at a time, while whisking. Continue mixing until blended. Add in powdered sugar and vanilla. Blend until frosting is completely mixed. Spread frosting over brownie top. Slice and serve.

ROCKY ROAD *Brownies*

Fill your brownies with almonds for a crunch. Then top them with marshmallow, almonds, and chocolate chips for a rich rocky road brownie.

Serves · 15–18

1 (18-oz.) box brownie mix

additional ingredients as listed on back of brownie mix (eggs, oil, water)

½ cup chopped almonds (or other nut)

FOR THE TOPPING:

2½ cups mini marshmallows

¼ cup chopped almonds

¼ cup milk chocolate chips

PREHEAT OVEN AND PREPARE BROWNIE BATTER according to package directions. Add chopped almonds to batter and stir in. Pour batter into a greased 9 × 13 pan and bake according to package directions.

Sprinkle marshmallows over the top of brownies and return to oven for 1–2 minutes until marshmallows just start to melt. Remove from oven and sprinkle with chocolate chips and chopped almonds. Allow to cool and then slice and serve.

tip: *The gooey marshmallows may be hard to slice up cleanly. Dip your knife into warm water between each slice, or coat your knife lightly in nonstick cooking spray.*

SLOW COOKER MOLTEN LAVA
Brownies

For an easy dessert, make these molten lava brownies in your slow cooker. Gooey pudding brownies topped with ice cream make for an amazing dessert.

Serves · 10–12

1 (18-oz.) box brownie mix

eggs and oil as listed
on back of brownie mix

milk (instead of water called for
on the box, use the same amount
of milk)

1 (3.9-oz.) pkg. instant chocolate
pudding

2 cups milk

ice cream, optional

SPRAY A LARGE SLOW COOKER WITH NONSTICK SPRAY.

Combine brownie mix with eggs, oil, and milk. Pour batter into prepared slow cooker.

Stir together pudding and milk until smooth. Pour carefully over brownie batter in slow cooker.

Cover slow cooker with a paper towel (to catch the condensation) and cover with lid. Cook on high for 2–3 hours, checking every 20 minutes after 2 hours until done. Some pudding will stay on the top and still look wet, so watch for when the edges look dry and done.

Serve warm with ice cream if desired.

TRIPLE PEANUT BUTTER
Brownies

These brownies are packed full of peanut butter, peanut butter cups, and peanut butter baking chips for the ultimate brownie for peanut butter chocolate lovers.

Serves ·15–18

1 (18-oz.) box brownie mix

additional ingredients as listed on back of brownie mix (eggs, oil, water)

½ cup peanut butter chips

½ cup chopped peanut butter cups

¼ cup peanut butter

PREHEAT OVEN AND PREPARE BROWNIE BATTER according to package directions. Mix in peanut butter chips and chopped peanut butter cups. Pour mixture into a greased 9 × 13 pan.

Melt peanut butter in a small bowl in the microwave for 30 seconds. Stir until it is nice and creamy. Spoon peanut butter in fourths on top of brownie batter. Using a knife, swirl peanut butter and brownie batter together, creating a marbled effect.

Bake for 32–35 minutes, until an inserted toothpick comes out mostly clean.

Zucchini BROWNIES

Add a little shredded zucchini to your brownies to get your kids to eat their vegetables. They won't even notice the difference in these delicious chocolate treats!

Serves · 15–18

1 (18-oz.) box brownie mix

eggs and water as listed
on back of brownie mix

half the amount of oil as
listed on back of brownie mix

applesauce, same amount as oil

1½ cups shredded zucchini

FOR THE CHOCOLATE
FROSTING (OPTIONAL):

½ cup butter (1 stick), softened

$1/3$ cup cocoa powder

2½ cups powdered sugar

$1/3$ cup whipping cream or half and
half

PREHEAT OVEN ACCORDING TO PACKAGE DIRECTIONS. Combine brownie mix, eggs, water, oil, and applesauce. Fold shredded zucchini into brownie batter. Pour batter into a greased 9 × 13 pan. Bake for 30–35 minutes, until a toothpick comes out clean. Allow to cool completely.

FOR CHOCOLATE FROSTING: Cream butter in a medium-sized bowl until smooth. Add in cocoa powder, powdered sugar, and cream. Once everything is combined, continue whipping frosting for about 3 minutes until light and fluffy.

Spread frosting over brownies. Allow to set for a few minutes, and then slice up and serve.

Skillet BROWNIES

A delicious, fudgy, hot, and gooey brownie topped with ice cream is about as good as it gets.

Serves · 4–6

¾ cup brownie mix (not prepared)

1 egg yolk

2 Tbsp. oil

1 Tbsp. water

2 Tbsp. chocolate chips

2 scoops ice cream

PREHEAT OVEN TO 350 DEGREES. In a small bowl, combine brownie mix, egg yolk, oil, and water until combined.

Pour mixture into a greased 8-inch cast iron skillet. Sprinkle chocolate chips on top and place in oven for 14–15 minutes.

Allow to cool for 2–3 minutes before topping with ice cream and serving!

Turtle BROWNIES

These brownies have the same great flavors as your favorite turtle candies, with pecans, caramel and chocolate.

Serves · 15–18

1 (18-oz.) box brownie mix

eggs, oil, and water listed on back of brownie mix

½ cup chopped pecans

1 cup chopped Rolo candy

FOR THE TOP OF THE BROWNIES:

¼ cup chopped pecans

¼ cup chopped Rolo candy

PREHEAT OVEN AND PREPARE BROWNIE batter according to package directions. Mix ½ cup pecans and 1 cup Rolo pieces into brownie batter. Pour batter into a greased 9 × 13 pan. Bake brownies for 28–32 minutes, until a toothpick inserted comes out mostly clean.

Remove brownies from oven and sprinkle ¼ cup chopped pecans and ¼ cup chopped Rolos over brownie top.

tip: Try topping the brownies with coarse sea salt when they are done baking as well, for a perfect sweet and salty treat.

BROWNIE
Batter Desserts

Brownie Batter DIP

This creamy, chocolatey brownie batter dip is perfect served with pretzels, graham crackers, cookies, fruit, and more. Its egg-free, so it is great for those with egg allergies or anyone who just loves the taste of brownie batter. This dip makes a lot so be sure to make it for a party, potluck, or game night with friends.

1 (8-oz.) pkg. cream cheese, softened

8 oz. Cool Whip

1 (18-oz.) box brownie mix, dry

2 Tbsp. milk

1 cup mini chocolate chips, optional

OPTIONAL DIPPERS:

mini pretzels

graham crackers

chopped fruit

cookies

CREAM TOGETHER CREAM CHEESE AND COOL WHIP in a large mixing bowl. Add in brownie mix and milk. Stir until everything is smooth. Mix in chocolate chips if desired.

Store in fridge until you're ready to serve. Serve with whatever you want to dip in it—cookies, fruit, pretzels, and so on.

tip: This recipe can be easily halved. Use 1½ cups brownie mix, 4 oz. cream cheese, 4 oz. Cool Whip, 1 Tbsp. milk, and ½ cup mini chocolate chips.

Brownie Batter
MILKSHAKE

Enjoy the great taste of brownie batter in milkshake form. This easy-to-make milkshake is the perfect treat for one, or two.

Serves · 1–2

1½ cups ice cream, chocolate or vanilla

½ cup milk

¼ cup + 2 Tbsp. brownie mix, dry

OPTIONAL TOPPINGS:

1 (8-oz.) container Cool Whip, or 2 cups whipped cream

chocolate syrup

brownie pieces

ADD ICE CREAM, MILK, AND BROWNIE MIX to a blender and mix until smooth.

Pour into a large glass and top with whipped cream, chocolate syrup, and brownie pieces if desired.

Brownie Batter BARK

This subtly brownie-flavored bark is a delicious treat to eat or share with neighbors.

Serves · 15–20

1½ cups milk chocolate chips

3 Tbsp. brownie mix (not prepared)

½ cup white chocolate chips

sprinkles, optional

PUT MILK CHOCOLATE CHIPS into a medium-sized bowl and microwave in 20-second increments, stirring after each, until smooth, about 1 minute total. Pour brownie mix into chocolate, 1 tablespoon at a time, stirring until smooth after each addition. Pour chocolate onto a baking sheet lined with parchment paper or a silicone liner and spread smooth to desired thickness.

Microwave white chocolate chips in a medium-sized bowl in 20-second increments, stirring after each, until smooth, about 1 minute total. Scoop white chocolate by spoonfuls onto milk chocolate and, using a knife or a toothpick, swirl around to create a marbled effect. Top with sprinkles if desired.

Allow to harden at room temperature until chocolate is completely cooled and hard. Break into pieces and serve.

Brownie Batter FROSTING

This creamy brownie batter frosting is perfect on top of cookies, cupcakes, or cake.

½ cup butter (1 stick), softened

3 Tbsp. milk

½ cup brownie
mix, (not prepared)

2½–3 cups powdered sugar

IN A LARGE MIXING BOWL, CREAM BUTTER UNTIL LIGHT AND FLUFFY.

Add milk and brownie mix to butter and stir in completely.

Slowly add powdered sugar into mixture while stirring. Add a little more milk or a little more powdered sugar to get desired consistency. Whip for a few minutes until frosting is light and fluffy.

Serve frosting on cookies, cupcakes, and so on.

Brownie Batter FUDGE

This creamy and smooth fudge is laced with a subtle chocolate brownie flavor for a fun treat.

Serves · 30–36, 2 pieces per person

1 (7-oz.) container marshmallow crème

1½ cups white sugar

1 (5-oz.) can evaporated milk

¼ cup butter (½ stick)

¼ tsp. salt

1½ tsp. vanilla extract

2 cups chocolate chips

½ cup brownie mix (not prepared)

IN A MEDIUM-SIZED POT, COMBINE marshmallow crème, sugar, evaporated milk, butter, and salt over medium heat.

Bring to a boil while stirring regularly. Once boiling, set a timer for 5 minutes and stir constantly. Remove from heat.

Add in vanilla, chocolate chips, and brownie mix. Stir everything together until smooth.

Pour mixture into a lightly greased 9 × 9 or 11 × 7 baking dish. Spread top evenly to smooth.

Place fudge in fridge to chill for 2 hours. Slice into pieces and serve.

Brownie Batter
MINI CHEESECAKES

These mini cheesecakes have a delicious chocolate cookie crust and a creamy brownie batter cheesecake filling, and they can be topped with chocolate syrup and strawberries for the perfect chocolate and berry combination.

Serves · 12

1 (8-oz.) pkg. cream cheese, room temperature

2 Tbsp. sugar

2 Tbsp. sour cream

2 Tbsp. heavy cream

1 dash salt

½ cup brownie mix, (not prepared)

½ tsp. vanilla extract

1 egg, room temperature

FOR THE CRUST:

14 chocolate crème-filled cookies

1 Tbsp. brownie mix, dry (not prepared)

3 Tbsp. butter, melted

OPTIONAL TOPPINGS:

chocolate syrup

sliced strawberries

PREHEAT OVEN TO 350 DEGREES. Place 12 cupcake liners into a regular muffin tin.

FOR CRUST: Pulse chocolate cookies in a blender to a fine crumb. Pour into a bowl and stir in brownie mix. Add in melted butter and stir together. Scoop about 1 tablespoon crumb mixture into each cupcake liner. Press down with a spoon. Bake crust in preheated oven for 6 minutes. Allow crust to cool for a few minutes when done.

FOR CHEESECAKE FILLING: In a large stand mixer, beat cream cheese until smooth. Add in sugar, sour cream, heavy cream, salt, and brownie mix and stir for about 2 minutes until fully combined. Add in vanilla and egg. Mix until just combined. Scoop 1 heaping tablespoon over each cookie crust, until all batter is used and distributed evenly. Bake cheesecakes for about 20 minutes, tops should be mostly set but may jiggle a little still.

Allow cheesecakes to cool at room temperature for 1 hour and then place in fridge and chill for another hour.

Top each cheesecake with chocolate syrup and strawberries if desired.

Brownie Batter
MUDDY BUDDIES

Add brownie batter and brownie pieces for a delicious twist to this favorite tasty treat. This is perfect for snacking during a movie night, game night, or when you just need a little something sweet.

Serves · 10–14

1½ cups chocolate chips

6 cups Chex cereal

1 cup brownie mix, (not prepared)

¼ cup powdered sugar

1–2 cups chopped brownie pieces (optional)

PUT CHOCOLATE CHIPS IN A SMALL MICROWAVE-SAFE BOWL. Melt them in microwave for about 1 minute on 50 percent power. Stir chocolate. Melt for additional 30-second increments on 50 percent power until completely smooth.

Pour melted chocolate over Chex cereal in a large bowl and stir together.

Pour chocolate-covered cereal into a gallon-sized ziplock bag. Dump in brownie mix and powdered sugar. Shake until cereal is completely coated. Add in brownie pieces if desired. Pour into a bowl and enjoy.

Brownie Mix
BANANA BREAD

Using a brownie mix to make banana bread gives it such a nice, rich chocolate flavor

Serves · 8–10

2 large bananas (1 cup mashed)

1/3 cup oil

3 eggs

1 (18-oz.) box brownie mix

1 cup chocolate chips *

1 tsp. flour

PREHEAT OVEN TO 350 DEGREES. In a large bowl, mash bananas with a fork. Mix in oil and eggs. Add in brownie mix and stir until just combined. Fold chocolate chips into batter.

Pour batter into a greased 9 × 5 bread pan. Bake for 50–60 minutes until a toothpick inserted comes out mostly clean. Allow bread to cool in pan for 15 minutes. Run a knife around pan edge and invert pan to get bread out. Cool bread completely on a cooling rack before slicing.

* Chocolate chips should be folded into the batter carefully, not stirred, to keep them from sinking to the bottom.

tip: Coat chocolate chips in about 1 tsp. flour in a small bowl. This will help prevent them from all sinking to the bottom of the bread.

BROWNIE BATTER
Pretzel Bites

These delicious bites are the perfect sweet and salty treat. With eggless brownie batter dough stuffed between two salty pretzels, and then dipped in chocolate, you won't be able to keep your hands off of these.

Serves · 35

1½ cups brownie
mix (not prepared)

¼ cup butter (½ stick), melted

1½ Tbsp. milk

about 70 mini pretzels

1 cup chocolate chips (or
½ cup chocolate chips,
½ cup white chocolate chips)

sprinkles, optional

IN A MEDIUM-SIZED BOWL, combine the brownie mix, butter and milk together to form a thick, soft dough. Add in a little more brownie batter or milk if needed to get the dough to a good, thick consistency.

Line a baking pan with parchment paper. Roll brownie batter dough into balls, 1 to 1½ teaspoons in size. Press 1 dough ball onto a mini pretzel and top with a second pretzel. Repeat until all batter and all pretzels have been used. Place in freezer for about 30 minutes.

Place chocolate chips into a small bowl (or 1 bowl for white chocolate chips and 1 for chocolate chips if doing half and half). Microwave in 20-second increments, stirring after each increment, about 1 minute total, until the chocolate is smooth and creamy. Dip pretzel bites halfway into chocolate or halfway into white chocolate and place back on parchment paper. Top with sprinkles if desired. Rest on parchment paper at room temperature until chocolate is hardened.

Brownie Batter
RICE KRISPIE TREATS

Enjoy the great taste of brownie batter mixed with gooey marshmallows with this fun twist on rice krispie treats. Stuff them full of brownie pieces for an even richer flavor.

Serves · 24

¼ cup butter (½ stick)

5 cups mini marshmallows

¾ cup brownie mix (not prepared)

5 cups chocolate crispy rice cereal

2 cups chopped brownie bites (optional)

MELT BUTTER IN A LARGE POT OVER MEDIUM-LOW HEAT. Add in mini marshmallows and allow them to melt, stirring constantly. Add in brownie mix and stir into marshmallows until combined.

Dump in rice cereal and brownie bits. Mix everything together until cereal is covered with marshmallow mixture. Remove from heat.

Pour rice krispie treats into a greased 9 × 13 pan. Carefully press rice krispie treats down evenly with a rubber spatula. Allow rice krispie treats to cool before cutting into pieces and serving.

BROWNIE *Batter* PANCAKES

These chocolatey pancakes are great for breakfast, or dessert. They're perfect for a birthday celebration, or any occasion. Top them with whipped cream, chocolate, and sprinkles to make them even more special!

1 cup brownie mix, (not prepared)

1 cup Bisquick pancake mix, or other dry pancake mix

2 eggs

½ cup milk

OPTIONAL TOPPINGS:

chocolate syrup

whipped cream

sprinkles

PREHEAT AN ELECTRIC GRIDDLE OR PAN TO 350 DEGREES, or medium-high heat.

In a large bowl, stir together brownie mix and pancake mix. Add in eggs and milk and stir until just combined.

Using a ¼-cup measuring cup, scoop pancake batter onto griddle. Allow to cook until pancake has bubbles across its top. Flip and cook another couple minutes until its bottom is cooked and pancake is cooked through.

Top pancakes with whipped cream, chocolate syrup, and sprinkles, as desired.

BROWNIE *Cinnamon Rolls*

Add a delicious chocolate twist to cinnamon rolls with these brownie sweet rolls. They're perfect for breakfast or dessert!

Serves · 12–15

2 yeast packets (or 5½ tsp. – each packet contains 2¼ tsp.)

1 cup warm milk

2 eggs

½ tsp. salt

¼ cup butter (½ stick)

4 cups flour

2 cups brownie mix (not prepared)

FOR THE FILLING:

¹/₃ cup butter

1 cup brown sugar

2 Tbsp. cinnamon

1 cup mini chocolate chips

FOR THE CREAM CHEESE FROSTING:

1 (8-oz.) pkg. softened cream cheese

½ cup butter (1 stick), softened

1½ cups powdered sugar

1 tsp. vanilla extract

DISSOLVE YEAST IN WARM MILK IN A LARGE BOWL. Add in eggs, salt, butter, flour, and brownie mix. Mix well. Once dough starts to come away from the edges, knead for 5 minutes (if you use your hands, dust them with flour to avoid sticking) until a large ball is formed. Cover the bowl with a towel and allow to rise for 45 minutes to 1 hour, until dough has doubled in size. Punch down dough slightly.

Lightly flour a counter top and roll dough out into a rectangle about ¼–inch thick.

Preheat oven to 400 degrees.

Melt butter for the filling. Combine brown sugar and cinnamon in a small bowl. Spread butter over dough surface. Sprinkle cinnamon sugar mixture generously over dough surface. Sprinkle mini chocolate chips over cinnamon sugar mixture.

Carefully roll dough from long top edge to bottom edge. Using thread or a very sharp knife, cut dough into 1-inch slices.

Lightly grease a 9 × 13 baking pan. Rolls might not all fit in pan, so use a bread pan or 8-inch square pan for additional rolls. Place rolls in baking pan and bake for 14–15 minutes.

While rolls are baking, make the frosting. Beat cream cheese until smooth. Add in butter and mix until blended. Add in powdered sugar and vanilla, and then continue to mix until blended.

Remove rolls from oven and allow to cool for about 5 minutes before frosting. Apply frosting generously to rolls.

NO CHURN *Brownie Batter* ICE CREAM

This delicious and creamy brownie-batter-flavored ice cream, full of mini chocolate chips, is easy to make—you don't even need an ice cream maker.

2 cups heavy whipping cream

1 (14-oz.) can sweetened condensed milk

1 cup brownie mix, dry (not prepared

2 Tbsp. cocoa powder

½ cup mini chocolate chips

IN A LARGE MIXING BOWL, whip the heavy cream over high speed until stiff peaks start to form. (Don't overmix or you'll make butter.)

In another bowl combine the sweetened condensed milk, brownie mix, cocoa powder, and chocolate chips.

Pour the whipped cream into the sweetened condensed milk mixture and fold them together until just combined. Pour into a three-quart can and cover tightly.

Place in the freezer for 6 hours, up to overnight, before serving.

BROWNIE Mix-Ins

Brownie
ICE CREAM SUNDAES

Enjoy the sweet combo of brownies and ice cream with these amazing brownie ice cream sundaes. Warm brownies topped with cold ice cream and your choice of ice cream toppings makes a delicious treat!

Serves · 12–15

1 (18-oz.) box brownie mix
additional ingredients as listed on back of brownie mix (eggs, oil, water)

FOR THE ICE CREAM SUNDAE:

1 (½-qt.) carton of ice cream (any flavor)

OPTIONAL TOPPINGS:

chocolate syrup

caramel syrup

peanut butter

chopped strawberries, bananas, cherries, and so on

sprinkles

PREHEAT OVEN, PREPARE BROWNIE BATTER, and bake brownies according to package directions in a greased 9 × 13 pan. Remove from oven and slice brownies into 12–15 pieces. Or allow brownies to cool completely before slicing and using.

Put 1 brownie on a plate or in a bowl and top with 1 or 2 scoops of ice cream. Drizzle chocolate syrup, caramel, peanut butter, chopped fruit, sprinkles, or any other toppings over the ice cream and brownie as desired.

Brownie KEBABS

The brownie kebab is the perfect summertime treat with brownies, strawberries, and marshmallows all drizzled with chocolate.

Serves · 32

1 (18-oz.) box brownie mix
additional ingredients as listed on back of brownie mix (eggs, oil, water)

FOR THE KEBABS:

about 1 (10.5-oz.) bag large marshmallows

64 strawberries, rinsed and greens cut off

32 wooden skewers

½ cup chocolate chips

PREHEAT OVEN, PREPARE BROWNIE BATTER, and bake brownies according to package directions in a greased 8 × 8 or 9 × 9 baking pan. Remove from oven and allow brownies to cool completely. Cut brownies into 1-inch squares and place in fridge to chill for at least 1 hour.

Thread wooden skewers, alternating with brownies, fruit, and marshmallows.

Place chocolate chips in a medium-sized bowl in the microwave. Melt in 20-second increments, stirring after each one, about 1 minute total, until smooth and creamy. Put chocolate into a small ziplock bag and clip a tiny bit of one corner off. Drizzle chocolate over each kebab. Return kebabs to fridge to allow chocolate to harden until ready to serve.

Brownie
ICE CREAM SANDWICHES

Creamy ice cream sandwiched between rich and fudgy chocolate brownies makes an even more decadent ice cream sandwich dessert!

Serves · 12–16

1 (18-oz.) box brownie mix
additional ingredients as listed on back of brownie mix (eggs, oil, water)

½ (1.5-qt.) carton vanilla ice cream (or any flavor)

PREHEAT OVEN AND PREPARE BROWNIE BATTER ACCORDING TO PACKAGE DIRECTIONS. Line two 8 × 8 or 9 × 9 square pans with foil or parchment paper carefully. Spray generously with nonstick spray. Pour half of brownie batter into each pan. Bake for 22–25 minutes, until a toothpick inserted comes out clean. Allow brownies to cool completely.

Let ice cream soften a bit, about 5 minutes. Spread ice cream over one pan of brownies. Carefully lift second pan of brownies out of the pan and remove foil/parchment and place brownies over ice cream layer. Cover pan with plastic wrap and freeze for 2 hours or longer.

Slice into pieces and wrap each brownie ice cream sandwich individually in plastic wrap and refreeze for 1 hour (or up to overnight) before serving.

Brownie-Stuffed
CHOCOLATE CHIP COOKIES

A delicious fudgy brownie stuffed inside a chocolate chip cookie combines the best of both worlds for an ultra chocolatey and delicious dessert.

Serves · 25

1 (18-oz.) box brownie mix
additional ingredients as listed on back of brownie mix (eggs, oil, water)

FOR THE CHOCOLATE CHIP COOKIES:

1 cup butter (2 sticks), softened

½ cup sugar

1 cup brown sugar

2 tsp. vanilla extract

2 large eggs

1 tsp. baking soda

1 tsp. salt

3 cups flour

2 cups chocolate chips

PREHEAT OVEN, PREPARE BROWNIE BATTER, and bake brownies in a greased 9 × 9 pan according to package directions. Remove from oven and allow brownies to cool completely.

Cut hard edges off of brownies. Cut brownies into 1½-inch squares (or 5 × 5) to get 25 brownie pieces.

Preheat oven to 350 degrees. In a large bowl, cream together butter and sugars until light, about 2 minutes. Add in vanilla and eggs. Stir until combined. In a separate bowl, combine baking soda, salt, and flour. Add these into wet mixture and stir everything together until just combined. Fold in chocolate chips.

Scoop out 2 separate tablespoons of cookie dough and flatten each with your hands. Place a brownie square on top of 1 piece of cookie dough and place the second piece of dough on top. Pinch cookie dough edges closed, sealing brownie square in the middle. Repeat with additional dough and brownies. Place 6–8 cookies onto a baking sheet lined with parchment paper or a silicone liner and flatten slightly.

Bake in oven for about 13 minutes, or until the cookie just starts to turn golden on the edges. Allow to cool on pan for 3–4 minutes before moving to cooling rack to cool completely.

Brownie TRIFLE CUPS

Delicious personal-sized trifles, with layers of brownies, pudding, and whipped cream, all topped with fresh raspberries.

Serves · 8

1 (18-oz.) box brownie mix
additional ingredients as listed on back of brownie mix (eggs, oil, water)

FOR THE TRIFLE CUPS:

1 (3.9-oz.) box instant chocolate pudding

2 cups cold whole milk

8 (½-pt.) mason jars

1½ cups whipped cream (4 oz.)

1 cup fresh raspberries

PREHEAT OVEN, PREPARE BROWNIE BATTER, and bake brownies in a greased 9 × 13 pan according to package directions. Remove from oven and allow brownies to cool completely. Set half of brownies aside for another use.

Whisk pudding together with whole milk in a large bowl using a hand mixer or stand mixer on slow for 2 minutes. Place in fridge and allow to set for 1 hour.

Cut half pan of brownies into small 1-centimeter- to ½-inch-sized cube pieces.

Scoop 3 tablespoons prepared pudding into the bottom of each mason jar. Scoop 2 tablespoons whipped cream on top of pudding. Sprinkle ¼ cup brownie pieces on top of each jar's whipped cream. Repeat process with another layer of pudding and whipped cream. Top each trifle with fresh raspberries.

tip: This recipe only uses ½ pan brownies. Double pudding, milk, whipped cream, and raspberries to use entire pan of brownies. Or enjoy extra brownies plain or in another recipe.

Brownie ICE CREAM CAKE

Even better than a scoop of ice cream on top of a brownie, this brownie ice cream cake has two layers of brownie and two layers of ice cream, all topped with chocolate syrup and fresh strawberries or any other topping. This cake is great for birthdays, parties, or any time!

Serves · 12–16

1 (18-oz.) box brownie mix
additional ingredients as listed on back of brownie mix (eggs, oil, water)

2 qts. ice cream (any flavor)

PREHEAT OVEN AND PREPARE BROWNIE BATTER ACCORDING TO PACKAGE DIRECTIONS. Line two 8- or 9-inch round pans with foil and spray generously with nonstick spray. Pour half of brownie batter into each pan. Bake for 18–22 minutes, until a toothpick inserted comes out clean. Allow brownies to cool completely.

Let ice cream soften a bit, about 5 minutes. Spread half of ice cream over one pan of brownies. Carefully lift second pan of brownies out of the pan and remove foil and place brownies over ice cream layer. Spread remaining ice cream over brownie layer and cover pan with plastic wrap. Freeze for 2 hours or longer.

Drizzle chocolate syrup over cake and top with strawberries or other choice of topping. Slice into pieces and serve.

Brownie ON A STICK

Eating brownies off of a stick and covered in chocolate and sprinkles is the perfect treat that both kids and adults will love.

Serves · 15

1 (18-oz.) box brownie mix
additional ingredients as listed on back of brownie mix (eggs, oil, water)

FOR THE STICKS:

15 popsicle sticks

1½ cups chocolate chips (or white chocolate chips)

sprinkles

PREHEAT OVEN, PREPARE BROWNIE BATTER, and bake brownies in an 8 × 8 pan according to package directions. Remove from oven and cover. Place brownies in fridge for about 1 hour to cool.

Cut brownies into 15 pieces and stick popsicle sticks into the ends of each brownie piece. Return to fridge for 1 hour.

Place chocolate chips in a medium-sized bowl in the microwave. Melt in 20-second increments, stirring after each one, about 1 minute total, until smooth and creamy. Dip brownies into chocolate, about halfway in, and then place on waxed paper. Cover tops with sprinkles. Return to fridge for about 30 minutes and then enjoy!

Brownie TRUFFLES

An easy homemade brownie rolled up with cream cheese and dipped in chocolate for the perfect little bite-sized treats.

Serves · 40–45

1 (18-oz.) box dry brownie mix

additional ingredients as listed on back of brownie mix (eggs, oil, water)

2 Tbsp. cream cheese

2 cups chocolate chips

PREHEAT OVEN, PREPARE BROWNIE BATTER, and bake brownies in a greased 9 × 13 pan according to package directions. Remove from oven and allow brownies to cool completely. Cut hard edges off of brownies and set aside or discard.

Scoop cooked brownie middle into a large bowl with cream cheese and stir to combine.

Roll brownie mixture into balls and place on a cookie sheet lined with parchment paper. Place in freezer for about 30 minutes, until firm.

Place chocolate chips in a medium-sized bowl in the microwave. Melt in 20-second increments, about 1 minute total, stirring after each until smooth. Dip each truffle ball into chocolate using a toothpick and place back on parchment paper. Allow chocolate to set completely. Before chocolate sets, you can top with sprinkles, or after it has set you can drizzle with additional chocolate for desired looks.

Other BROWNIE Delights

Brownie FRUIT PIZZA

Make this chocolatey dessert pizza with a creamy frosting and fresh fruit for a sweet and delicious treat. Perfect for a crowd.

Serves · 16

1 (18-oz.) box brownie mix
additional ingredients as listed on back of brownie mix (eggs, oil, water)

FOR THE FROSTING:

4 oz. cream cheese

4 oz. Cool Whip

2 cups powdered sugar

FOR THE TOPPINGS:

1 (11-oz.) can mandarin oranges

about 8 strawberries

4 kiwi

¼ cup blueberries

PREHEAT OVEN AND PREPARE BROWNIE BATTER according to package directions. Spray a 14-inch pizza pan (not deep dish) with nonstick spray, and sprinkle with flour. Pour brownie batter into prepared pan. Bake for about 16 minutes until a toothpick inserted comes out clean. Allow brownie pizza to cool.

Combine frosting ingredients in a small bowl until smooth. Spread frosting over brownie pizza top.

Rinse and dry fruit completely. Drain mandarin oranges. Slice strawberries. Peel kiwi and slice into circles. Arrange fruit over fruit pizza top in any pattern to cover pizza completely. Slice pizza into 16 pieces and serve.

Brownie-Swirled
YELLOW CAKE

By combining brownie batter and cake batter, you'll get a delicious chocolate and yellow swirled cake. This cake has bites of rich fudgy brownie with warm buttery cake to make the perfect cake for any occasion.

Serves · 15–18

1 (18-oz.) box brownie mix

additional ingredients as listed on back of brownie mix (eggs, oil, water)

1 extra egg (for cake-like brownies)

1 (15-oz.) box yellow cake mix

water, oil, and eggs as listed on back of cake mix, less ¼ cup water

1 (16-oz.) can chocolate frosting, or 2 cups favorite homemade chocolate frosting

PREHEAT OVEN TO 350 DEGREES. In a large bowl, combine brownie mix with water, oil, and eggs listed on the back of the box for cake-like brownies. Set it aside. In another large bowl, combine cake mix with water (¼ cup less than called for), oil, and eggs as listed on the back of the box. Set cake batter aside too.

Pour ⅔ of brownie batter into a greased 9 × 13 pan. Pour cake batter over brownie batter. Drop remaining brownie batter by spoonfuls on top of cake batter. Using a knife to swirl batter back and forth across cake, create a marbled effect over its top.

Bake for 45–50 minutes, until a toothpick inserted comes out clean, or the cake bounces back when you press it with your finger. Allow cake to cool completely.

Spread frosting over cake top, slice into pieces, and serve.

Brownie CHOCOLATE CHIP COOKIES

Now instead of having to decide between brownies or cookies for dessert, you can have both!

Serves · 24

1 (18-oz.) box brownie mix

1 large egg

$1/3$ cup oil

2 Tbsp. water

$1/4$ cup flour

1 cup chocolate chips

PREHEAT OVEN TO 350 DEGREES. Combine brownie mix, egg, oil, water, flour, and chocolate chips in a large bowl.

Using a #40 cookie scoop (or a spoon), scoop twelve 1½-tablespoon-sized cookies onto a cookie sheet lined with parchment paper or a silicone liner.

Bake for 8–12 minutes until cookies start to set. Remove from oven and let cookies rest on baking sheet for 4–5 minutes. Remove to a cooling rack to cool completely. Repeat with remaining cookie dough on a cooled cookie sheet.

Brookies

This dessert gives you the best of both worlds, combining a brownie cookie and a chocolate chip cookie together. These soft cookies are rich, chewy, and totally addictive!

Serves · 36

CHOCOLATE CHIP COOKIE DOUGH:

½ cup butter (1 stick)

½ cup brown sugar

½ cup sugar

1 tsp. vanilla extract

1 egg

½ tsp. baking powder

½ tsp. baking soda

½ tsp. salt

1¾ cups flour

¾ cup chocolate chips

BROWNIE COOKIE DOUGH:

1 (18-oz.) box brownie mix

1 large egg

⅓ cup butter, softened

2 Tbsp. water

6 Tbsp. flour

¾ cup chocolate chips

START WITH MAKING CHOCOLATE CHIP COOKIE DOUGH. Cream butter and sugars together until light and fluffy. Stir in vanilla and egg. Dump in baking powder, baking soda, salt, and flour. Stir together. Fold in chocolate chips. Wrap in plastic wrap and place in fridge.

Combine brownie mix, egg, butter, water, and flour in a large bowl. Fold in chocolate chips. Wrap in plastic wrap and place in fridge until oven is fully preheated.

Preheat oven to 350 degrees.

Take 1 tablespoon of each cookie dough and push them together, roll them into a ball, and place them onto a cookie sheet lined with parchment paper or a silicone liner. Bake for 9–11 minutes until cookies are set and start to turn golden. Allow to cool for 4–5 minutes on the cookie sheet before removing to a cooling rack to cool completely.

Repeat with remaining cookie dough on a cooled cookie sheet.

Brownie BRITTLE

A crunchy, chocolate brownie brittle—the perfect chocolate treat.

Serves · 15–20

1½ cups brownie mix, dry

2 Tbsp. water

⅓ cup oil

1 egg

PREHEAT OVEN TO 325 DEGREES. Mix together brownie mix, water, oil, and egg in a medium-sized bowl.

Line a cookie sheet with parchment paper and spray with nonstick spray. Spread brownie batter evenly over parchment paper to cover two thirds of the pan.

Bake for 10 minutes. Rotate pan and bake for an additional 10 minutes.

Allow brownie brittle to cool completely before breaking into pieces.

Recipe Index

About the Author

Aimee Berrett is the cofounder of the popular website *Like Mother, Like Daughter*. She is a dessert junkie, a wife, and a mother. She married her husband in 2010 and wanted to try new dinner recipes. From there her love of cooking began. She started the food blog *Like Mother, Like Daughter* with her mom so they could share the recipes and food they loved despite living miles apart. Their recipes have been featured on multiple websites, including *Better Homes and Gardens*, Huffington Post, BuzzFeed, and *Deseret News*.

SCAN to visit

WWW.LMLD.ORG